Creating
Remarkable Results

Creating Remarkable Results

WISDOM FOR NAVIGATING THE COMPLEXITIES OF WORK & LIFE

Mary Mavis

Creating Remarkable Results / Mary Mavis. —1st ed.

Published by First Catch Press

Library of Congress Control Number: 2020947384

ISBN (paperback): 978-1-6629-0486-8
ISBN (eBook): 978-1-6629-0487-5

Dedicated to my son Michael and my grandchildren Julia, Charles, Winona, and Evangeline. A special gratitude to my husband Herb for being my partner in this remarkable life.

We are wiser than we know.
—Ralph Waldo Emerson

Contents

Foreword

By Bill Mezzanotte, Executive Vice President, Head Research & Development, and Chief Medical Officer at CSL Behring

Seek first to understand—then to be understood. This pithy axiom is Habit #5 of Steven Covey's famous *7 Habits of Highly Effective People,* and in a few words it elegantly summarizes the key to creating remarkable results at work and in life. To be the creator, you must first understand yourself and your world and how or why your idea is so meaningful and then, get really clear on the result you are hoping for. Psychologists and coaches alike have written about the unexplained power of full intentionality; that the act of writing down, with great specificity, your ambitions greatly increases the chances of those dreams being realized. Knowing what you want is an immense challenge—but of course, that is only the beginning. Then you must engage the world and often modify your vision with feedback from the world. The meeting of creativity and current reality can be painful. That is why it is often said that big organizations are where good ideas go to die. And the cause of death of these ideas is as much the individual creator as it is the organizational antibodies to the idea.

I left the clinical practice of medicine over twenty years ago in the hopes of making a bigger, more far-reaching impact on the health and lives of patients. I thought that just meant having the resources at hand to make my wonderful ideas a reality. Wrong! But through generous portions of humble pie, and the help of coaches like Mary, I have learned to create with others and have been fortunate enough to make the difference I hoped to make. And as I have graduated to higher positions of authority, influence, and mentorship, I have strived to help talented individuals on their own leadership journey to appreciate the complex interplay of knowing thy own self but also to know the environment in which they work and the importance of being purposeful in their interactions. When I fail, which is more often than I like to admit, I call Mary.

Mary has been helping me, the teams I work on, my peers, and the individuals and teams who work for me to achieve greater success. Her formula is both elegant and simple, just like Steven Covey's Habit #5: get people to understand what they want, why they are struggling, how the world perceives them and their ideas, and how they can change to achieve great results. Her principles are based on very foundational psychological principles and research, but her approach is completely non-academic and practical. She builds on individuals' skill bases and experiences, then artfully leads them through a journey of self, team, and organizational exploration that invariably leads to stronger, more sustained success. The principles Mary outlines in this book reflect the framework she utilizes and adjusts so that each individual grows—a thirteen-step recovery program if you will. As a mentor and a boss, I also learn something as a mentor every time Mary engages with one of my team members. I have seen her and her pupils in action now across three companies that I have been working for and watched in admiration as she applies gentle but constant traction to get my teams and leaders to stretch and change. Growth is hard work but easier when done gradually and purposefully rather than in one large crisis.

Internal consistency and authenticity are two really important values to me. In my own leadership, I have found that being internally and externally consistent makes life a lot easier; and leading as my authentic self takes a lot less energy than trying to pretend I am someone else. I tend to apply the same lens to other leaders with whom I engage: if you can't pull through what you say with how you act, or you want to pretend you are someone or something you are not, then I have precious little time for you and will have a hard time trusting you. Mary's style, in coaching and now writing, is a great example of consistency and authenticity. Mary teaches and coaches in a very unassuming way and even in this book undersells the exponential value of applying what seem like small changes in one's mindset and approach. And while she herself has grown and matured in our over-fifteen-year professional relationship, she is still fundamentally the same Mary Mavis I have always known, trusted, and admired, and her primary mission to help others succeed has never wavered.

For those individuals who are lucky enough to work with Mary, I encourage them to be open to the process, to reflect patiently and consistently on her advice, to celebrate the little wins in organizational effectiveness, and, importantly, to connect the small changes with their own change in approach. I encourage you, the reader, to do the same with this book—settle in to read it, either all at once, or in chapters, then reread it when situations arise at work or in life. Answer the questions that Mary poses. When something in the book clicks, or you enjoy a small win—celebrate it! Do not be fooled by the fact that the chapters are neither long nor dense. Albert Einstein once said, "If you can't explain it simply, you don't understand it well enough." Mary understands full well. All the content you need to create remarkable results at or outside your workplace is here if you can pay attention to the messages and reflect on their meaning to you and then try them in your own situation. I wish you good reading and good luck with your own remarkable journey toward the results you seek.

Acknowledgments

I cannot imagine a more satisfying experience than writing this book. It fulfills a decades-long goal of mine and, hopefully, will extend my reach to the next generation of leaders.

I've been privileged to work with so many smart, committed people in my career. Without their trust in my counsel, I would not have been able to develop and see the value of each principle in this book. In the sum total of principles, I hope to have honored those collaborations and each person's remarkable results.

There are so many people who have touched and influenced my work over the years. If you are not mentioned, please know that you are not forgotten. I want to give a special acknowledgment for their contribution to: Bill Mezzanotte and all my collaborators at CSL Behring; John O'Brien with whom I learned as much as I contributed and his co-creators at AstraZeneca; Abe Hughes and his teams at New Holland and Trimble; Monika Machon and her leadership teams when she was CIO and Treasurer at AIG; Rachel Biblow and our work at the Children's Hospital of Philadelphia; Pat Renzi at Milliman; Libby Keating, Doug Smith, Sandra Morgan, and my POET team at Janssen who sparked a cultural (r)evolution for early development teams: Stan Belkowski, David Blue,

Marc Ceusters, Moitreyee Chatterjee-Kishore, Darrel Pemberton, Ranabir SinhaRoy, and Marnix Van Loock.

Every entrepreneur has people in their professional network who fuel their thinking and encourage their work. Six particularly important people for me include: Wendy Axelrod, Shannon Breuer, Diane Brown, Karen Kaufman, Julian Kaufmann, and Tom Porter.

All of this thinking started with my Sibson & Company colleagues, an organization in which we created a remarkable culture together. A special mention for John Balkcom, Roger Brossy, Drueanne Heaney, Bill Hengen, Blair Jones, Dave Kuhlman, Lorri Perkins, Anne Saunier, Jane Shlaes, Steve Strelsin, and Glenn Wolfson. Even when the time is long between conversations, I always know you are there.

I am grateful to Mari Bernhagen, who was also a Sibson colleague and then my editor over the last twenty years. She was not only my technical editor for the book, but she has always been my cheerleader to get my ideas out in the world.

Most importantly, I want to acknowledge my husband, Herb Rappaport. In addition to his personal support in my perseverance to write this book, his broad knowledge and deep expertise as a PhD psychologist and business consultant has been invaluable to my thinking.

Introduction

Wisdom is a big word to attach to any person's ideas about the way things work and how people think and behave. I consider each concept in this book to be my own developed wisdom. I offer them as guiding principles for you to enhance your effectiveness in the most challenging situations and with the most interesting and complex people in your work life.

What are the complexities that you can expect to deal with at some point in your work? As a coach, I see at least five common themes:

1. A matrix or web of people with varying stakes in your desired or accountable result.
2. Ambiguous decisions, authority, and process.
3. People who "push your buttons" and seemingly create barriers to progress.
4. Slow traction in the critical work path, sometimes apathy in your function or teams or even senior leadership.
5. Legacy-protection often blocking progress or drifting into the way-we-were.

It may be hard to accept, but these and other realities are simply part of the working world. In this book, you will find a new way to step back, diagnose the situation and the people, relax your judgment, fuel your curiosity, and set out with your own clear intention to create.

In my work with clients, I have used the concept of targeting a "remarkable" result. By remarkable I mean exactly what you want to create. As part of my definition, remarkable results have a high degree of uncertainty and require you to take deliberate action in order to see what is possible. You will see that remarkable results can be big and small outcomes.

Wisdom crosses all bridges of life. I have always applied my thinking to both the work world and home. I've developed the thirteen principles in this book and helped and learned from my clients by translating the data from one environment to the other. At the heart of each environment, we bring ourselves and engage with others to produce results and experiences. Each principle applies in all realms of our lives.

My purpose in life and for this book is for you to achieve more of whatever you desire, whether a quantifiable outcome or a quality in your relationships or experiences. A remarkable life is as unique as one human being is to another. There is beauty in honoring and nurturing who you are and what you want.

Each chapter represents a core principle of mine, developed through my lens on people and life. My lens is shaped in part as a US-East Coast, college-educated, baby-boomer, army brat, white female, coach and consultant, and mother of a Generation Z son adopted from Russia.

I recognize that in another culture, time, and place, I might have developed different wisdom or the same with different experiences.

I have done my own deep work to understand myself and to consider and understand the people and world around me. I am humbled daily by the challenge of applying each wisdom and the vast reach and nuances of what I do not yet understand. While each principle may seem simple, the application in our most complex situations may not be.

While any person in the work world could get value from the book, you will see that many of the examples and focus are on the critical middle of the organizational hierarchy. These are the team leaders and department heads who bridge the effectiveness of senior leadership and the people who do the core work. That said, anyone, from top to bottom in the organization, can generate value from any or all of these concepts.

This book is not a "how to do" book, rather it is a "how to think" book. For many of the concepts, I have created "tools" and frameworks that may help you apply a particular wisdom to your work and life. The tools are designed to help you lay out your thinking and examples. You can peruse my Possibility Thinker Tools™ in the back of this book and download them from my website at www.maviscompany.com.

I intentionally wrote short chapters to capture the essence of each principle in the hope that the book could serve as a quick resource, as inspiration, or as a reminder that you can tuck into your backpack, briefcase, or handbag. You can start at any chapter that piques your interest.

> **Section One: Grounding** sets the stage for you as a creator, how you think about people in the world, and how you allow intended results to evolve naturally over time.
>
> **Section Two: Creation** takes you from creating an idea for a remarkable result to crystallizing your desired end-state.
>
> **Section Three: Challenges** covers some core beliefs that can free you from resistance, arrogance, and pessimism so that you can return to positive creating.
>
> **Section Four: Inspiration** covers one final chapter that hopes to fuel your creative confidence and energy for your remarkable results.

Some ideas may resonate with you immediately and deeply, while others seem foreign or opposite to your own experience. That's okay. I don't expect that you will agree with me on each one. However, I do hope that some will make you stop and think differently, see a new possibility, and try a new approach with success.

〜

I invite you to use my developed wisdom to enrich your own thinking and go beyond in your own way. All learning and results will manifest in your everyday life. And then, you become the remarkable part of my work!

> *"I am always doing that which I cannot do, in order that I may learn to do it."*
>
> *Pablo Picasso*

GROUNDING

GROUNDING

Be the creator of exactly what you want. If not you, then who? If not now, then when? It always starts with you!

1. You Are The Creator

You are the creator of your work and life: what you want to achieve…how you want to be as a person… with whom you choose to spend your time. You're the center and creator of your universe, in charge of living your present reality and designing your desired future. Now, is that a happy thought or a frightening one?

You Decide What You Want to Create

Are you the kind of person who always thinks big? Or, do you like simpler work and a modest life? Neither is better than the other, even if more TED Talks and books advise how to think big rather than how to create a simpler life.

At different junctures in your life you may desire different outcomes. It's a challenge and blessing when you are thinking for yourself—rather than thinking about and creating what you believe others expect and want for you.

3

You have the ability to decide to make changes in your life and work. If you can envision a different future and are willing to do the work to create it, you won't be limited by your history or personality. The work will require effort and learning, as well as internal reflection and perhaps rewiring. Rewiring is your chance to unravel any ingrained ways of thinking and then establish and practice new patterns.

Being a Creator Requires Perseverance

No matter your talents, you will encounter small, medium, and large problems along the way of life. You can't avoid them. What you can do is confront each problem knowing that you are strong and able to solve it on your own or with the help of others. You never need to watch passively as the circumstances of your life play out. You can always act. Here's proof:

> *After twelve years with a management consulting firm, I decided, in my forties, to launch my own firm. I knew more about building a consulting practice and had refined my way of creating a clear vision. I decided I would target a full backlog of work in three months. All my former colleagues thought I was crazy. At every turn I met people who "feared" for me, and I created a bit of my own fear. My mantra became "I want to work with people who will value my partnership*

*and work toward their goals." Despite the worries
of family, friends, and colleagues, I put my head
down every day and in three months looked up
to find that my goal was met.*

Pushing through fear and challenges is part of the equation of creating something remarkable. The time required is unpredictable—by nature. Therefore, your desire must exceed the challenge.

You Create In a Context with Limited Control

Every remarkable result is created in the context of the organization's culture, external climate, and synergies, strategies, or work underway. You are in control of your thinking and actions, but not in control of the people and world around you.

Goal setting at work is often a seesaw in which your boss wants you to reach for the remarkable; but they don't want to be on the hook for that result. You want to stretch your goals but don't want to fail to reach them. So, your human tendency can be to back into a less than remarkable target. But in this way, you misuse the context to shrink or prematurely alter your best thinking.

What would happen if you took two steps?

1. Target "exactly what you want," and
2. Set your formal performance objectives in line with the company's cascading objectives?

5

You can have your "back pocket" target without shooting yourself in the foot or scaring your management. In most organizations, your result will be rewarded whether you stated it in your goals or not.

One of my longest-running clients, let's call him Jerry, was the head of all early pharmaceutical products for a big pharma company. He was an amazing creator. In our work, I pushed him to think beyond his role and authority. It took a year for him to gauge leadership's readiness to "change the way the company developed drugs." Jerry had no charter or authority for that result. He had to create a clear vision of his desired end-state and then take actions and collaborate with colleagues who had final decision authority—but without them knowing his intention. His leadership team was aligned, keeping the goal in their collective back pocket, identifying the usual and unexpected opportunities to advance their result. Two years later, Jerry called me to share their success and an article in an industry periodical about "how they changed the way the company makes drugs." The success was over a significant time in the context of organization readiness, not within any performance cycle. The remarkable result was a highlight of Jerry's and his leaders' careers to-date.

Not all of your creating will end up with the outcomes you envision. You can only control your own way of thinking, behaving, and acting (and even that can be elusive). You may find impenetrable barriers as you work your plan. And, in some cases, you won't know enough when you're setting your sights.

The bottom line is that you never know what is possible until you set your mind and put the work into it.

Who You Surround Yourself with Matters

Remarkable results rarely, if ever, can be accomplished by you alone. Not only will you need some combination of partners, collaborators, sponsors, and followers, but you need people who see the possibilities you have envisioned and who will contribute, support, and cheer you on. You need the combined capabilities required for the result you have targeted. These are not just stakeholders; they are your co-creators. Co-creators are the people who participate, endorse, or benefit from your creation.

There are always naysayers and slow-downers to any remarkable goal (more on both in Almost Anything Is Possible). Rather than exclude or resist these people, think about them as useful to your planning and thinking. Engage them in dialogue. Learn from them. But, don't let them dissuade you from your true intended outcome—at least not without a challenge.

I began intentionally creating with a lot of encouragement from colleagues who cheered me on even

7

when my desired outcome seemed too unreasonable. Surround yourself with capable people who challenge you and, at the same time, lift you up.

～

I've learned that the creation process can be fun and inspiring, making you feel less at the mercy and whims of the people and world around you. It takes practice and reflection to see where you are positively creating, where you are potentially mis-creating, and how you are testing the limits to creating.

> *"Do you want to know what you are? You are a creator. At every moment you are creating. The real question is, what are you creating?"*
>
> *Bryant H. McGill, author, activist, and social entrepreneur*

Start Your Thinking

1. What desire will fuel your creating?
2. Have you considered yourself powerful enough to create a remarkable result?
3. If not you, then who? Why not now?

People are funny! Each and every one of us. Be an anthropologist. Observe with curiosity and genuine interest in understanding the person and the environment.

---

2. People Are Funny

F ew, if any of us, learned formally about the people side of work and life. They don't cover the topic in school. And at work, you learn that emotional intelligence is critical to success, yet knowing how to develop that type of intelligence may be a mystery. You watch and emulate people you respect and admire, and observe and complain about people you find difficult or different. Most of what you learn about people is general and based on superficial understanding. Even those who have deepened their understanding, if honest, would say they've only dealt with the tip of the iceberg. There is too much to know and understand, let alone being able to apply and use that understanding to your advantage.

Discover and Appreciate Each Person's Uniqueness

It sounds too simple to say that all individuals are unique. But it's true, and yet how often do you include that reality in your thinking? When differences butt up against your own approaches and thinking, you may get frustrated, angry, blaming, and (worst of all) sometimes you may withdraw. You can see a person as difficult, but I guarantee that someone else is equally frustrated with you.

If you want to do the hard task of creating results in your work and life, make the "soft stuff" interesting. Trying to truly understand people is not just complex, but also rewarding. The facts and observations that you gather over time form your database for understanding people. Rather than see a person as "difficult" (or something stronger), use the phrase *"people are funny."* That phrase can lead you toward more productive thinking about what you can do with a person who is *like that.* Consider this:

> *My son was adopted, and therefore we can't say he "gets it from Uncle Harry." He's a high-energy, creative, free spirit of a person. He's actually very powerful—and he knows it. He and I battled in his youth on every boundary that was set for him. He's not obedient and resists any control of his actions. I have come to understand over the years what he cares the most about—music, friends,*

and my loving support. I learned to build what
he cares about into the privileges in our home and
our relationship rather than make him wrong.
To this day, we rarely see life situations the same
way. But he says he knows that I understand him.
Decades of intentional interactions have paid off
in an open and connected relationship. He is in
his own life, and I am an important person in
that life—but not the creator.

Resistance Stops Your Thinking

When faced with a person who is different in ways that offend, you may resist engaging to understand. It is much more self-affirming to point the finger. That's human, unfortunately. The problem in resisting is that thinking stops. The brain freezes in judgment rather than opening with curiosity.

Over the years, I've had many clients at all organizational levels who report to bosses seen as "all about themselves." Most people greatly resist this type of person. How much more powerful is it to embrace the difference and use that understanding in how you engage that boss. Learn from "Lin":

One client, "Lin," reported to an executive who
was most interested in the results that would
give her personal success. That attitude, in turn,
caused Lin to withdraw and feel disdain for her.

Lin's intelligent mind had stopped thinking about anything other than how much she didn't like her boss.

When we laid out her boss's background and way of thinking (just the facts!), Lin saw how she could work with her boss's patterns and promote their common interests. She then started their meetings by focusing on her boss's biggest challenges and offering her help. What do you know, soon her boss had more time for Lin and welcomed the help from a very smart, senior leader direct report.

This leader created an easy entry to engage with a very different person, paving the way for new influence on key decisions.

Create Your People Database

What do you need to know about a person to be most influential or develop a good, productive, reciprocal relationship? Here are the Five Questions that I include as part of my "database" for people important to me.

Five Questions to Form Your Database

1. **What is FOUNDATIONAL in their background and experience?** From place of birth to

12

education to work experience, consider what in particular has been a critical part of the person's history and background.

2. **With what do they strongly IDENTIFY?** Everyone resonates with a particular role or segment of their work or personal life. For example, I identify with being a coach and a mother. It wouldn't take you long in knowing me to make that assessment.

3. **What KIND OF PERSON are they?** How do these individuals seem to think? What are their patterns of speech (something said often)? What are their typical ways of operating (e.g., communications, meetings, etc.)?

4. **What is IMPORTANT to them?** Think about what you know or what you might infer about what is important to them at work and at home. Is it a focus on results, process, customers, etc.? Think about the whole person; imagine how family, education, hobbies, etc. might be important.

5. **What INTERESTS them?** What topics, problems, or opportunities do they talk about with interest? Do you know anything about their continuing education interests or pastimes?

You will never have all the information about someone, not even a small fraction. Identify what you do know about the person; then notice what you don't know. Check your data for what you assume and what you actually know.

Add questions that will help you understand specific views or aspects across co-creators. For example, if you're trying to align on strategy, add a sixth question, such as:

1. "What have they said about the strategy?" or
2. "What are their interests in different strategic outcomes?" or
3. "Who are their key relationships (i.e., influencers, etc.)?"

Then look across your database for commonalities and differences. And look down and across an individual's data set.

For example, suppose your key person in question:

1. Is currently the department manager but spent twenty years in a competitor company that has a very different culture (**foundational**).
2. Seems very identified as an analyst and problem-solver, even though their role is a manager (**identity**).
3. Is the kind of person who broadly states expectations and seems annoyed when asked for clarity (**kind-of-person**).
4. Spends significant time with the boss and boss's boss—focused on political standing and

the success of the function's strategic goals (**importance**).

5. Talks sports, but you're not sure what business topics are of interest (**interests**).

Now suppose you have twenty years at the current company, have strong relationships across functions, and have a reputation for execution of complex work.

What approach would you use to gain trust, secure resources, or redirect the work plan? Clearly, any person is more complex than these five data points. But with this limited information, I might:

1. Offer my insights on the hierarchy of bosses and their peers, and

2. Tie my proposals to what those bosses consider important.

My suggestions above are not uncommon strategies in any hierarchy of decision-makers, but with this boss, they are critical.

Don't worry about whether you are exactly right about some of the data. It's **your** information; you're not going to publish it. But, make sure you consider what you know and what you are assuming or inferring. Most importantly, identify what you don't know and look for opportunities to add that information to your database.

You Are a Funny Person

Let's not forget that you are a funny person for some to many people. I see the funniness in my own behavior (ha-ha and not-so-ha-ha). I can tell a story on myself here.

> *For years, I led consulting teams that were scattered across the country, and each person worked on multiple projects for different project managers. Of course, I was very nice, smart, and considerate of my team members. I also drove them nuts by rethinking the plan or having a new idea two hours after a team meeting. As an extrovert who figures out what I think by talking it out, I am very comfortable iterating an idea or concept. For team members who were juggling competing deadlines, I could be a nightmare. What I learned over time was to make sure my teams knew what I knew about myself and that my pattern could cause problems for them. I also empowered them to stop me and tell me the consequences of any shifts I had in mind.*

Take some time to develop your profile of Five Questions. Isolate what you can tell people about working best with you, your strengths and your foibles—your funniness.

Multiple Co-Creators Heighten the Complexity

Thinking through one co-creator can be challenging enough, but what about the reality of multiple co-creators with diverse backgrounds and competing interests? For remarkable results, this complexity is a given. The Five Questions tool allows you to develop a table of information, starting with yourself. With that table, you can look across each question and at each profile to develop insights and ideas for your approach.

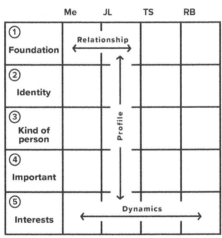

Look between, down, and across

Be an Anthropologist

An anthropologist is a scientist who studies human beings and their environments. To populate your database, you

17

would begin to observe a person's patterns of speech and behavior. You would ask questions about "how the person thinks" about a key issue and what the person's experience has been in similar situations. You would review LinkedIn profiles for clues to foundational experiences and what is important to the person, along with networks and any common contacts.

Imagine spending even 10 percent more time paying attention to the people side of the results equation. With a forty-hour workweek, you would invest one hour each day Monday through Thursday. With that investment, you will be far more able to engage and even orchestrate the field of play and players. And what could be more interesting than intentionally making an impact on your co-creators—the people who matter to your result.

〜

Understanding people (including ourselves) is a lifelong learning adventure. The personal value is unquestionable. I have found the phrase "people are funny" can be a reminder to shift from my critical judgment to my anthropologist's curiosity and a clear intention to make a bigger difference.

> *"Human beings are made up of many different values, and sometimes those values are in tension with each other."*
>
> *John Mackey, CEO of Whole Foods*

Start Your Thinking

1. Isolate a key decision that needs to be made at work or at home.
2. Lay out your profile and one or two key people to add to your database.
3. What ideas, insights, and missing data can you discern for each person and across profiles?

Use the Five Questions tool in the Possibility Thinker Tools™ at www.maviscompany.com.

Who said the world should be logical and "as we like it?" Embrace the craziness as part of reality.

3. The World Is Crazy

We think that logic, honesty, and justice should prevail. But check the news. Look around at your neighborhood or grocery store or our global cooperation on issues like climate change, poverty, and more. Take a look into world history and track how many wars, disputes, and practices made little sense then and make less sense now. Consider the wealth of your nation and at the same time the persistence of racism and inequality. Include the lack of readiness we had for a global health crisis.

Taking the craziness to organizations, I talk to many people who are angry or disheartened by the behaviors of leaders or decisions that are made. Companies reorganize year after year. Performance management is considered a waste of time and demotivating. Business decisions are seen as largely driven by the pursuit of personal gain.

BUT who said the world, organizations, and people should be logical and as we like it?

Crazy means something is "full of flaws" or lacks "sound reason." The world, countries, organizations, and families are all a bit crazy—in some way. If you honestly assess a person or organizing system (e.g., a city, institution, country), you will find flaws. When something is full of flaws, especially those you don't understand or don't like, you are more likely to use the word crazy. The bigger the problem, the bigger the impact. The bigger the impact, the crazier things can get.

Embrace Reality

You will resist crazy at first. You see actions or words that are not what you would do or say and add a jolt of emotion that sends your brain packing. It is human to object to decisions, injustices, turnabouts in direction—whatever you think either doesn't make sense or is wrong.

What if you learned to move with, around, or beyond the crazy in your world? This is hard, because the path forward requires you to embrace the reality of the craziness. By embrace, I don't mean agree with the craziness. Rather, I mean to accept the current state as the current state. Resistance, whether moving against or withdrawing from the reality, keeps you firmly embedded in crazy. The right type of embracing allows you to think more strategically or creatively, or let it go for another day, week, or quarter. Embracing reality gives you the opportunity to see what can be changed, evaluate possibilities, and move forward.

What can you do when faced with craziness?

Recognize Anxiety

When I see craziness, especially the kind that impedes my results, my anxiety goes way up. Often, my co-creators have the same reaction. When you have team members who are anxious, it is far more difficult to be productive.

Anxiety tends to attack the craziness. When a decision is made that spikes anxiety, it's common to point to someone or some group who is wrong to be so crazy. I can't tell you how many examples my clients have brought to our coaching. Over decades, here are some of the most common anxiety-producers:

1. A new organization structure for which the company cannot explain the "why" or the intended outcome.
2. A new boss who has no experience in the function or business when someone within the group has that expertise.
3. Your manager's manager has asked you to step up and help out when your manager leaves. You deliver on all the extra work. Then at performance review time, you find out that you are being rated a "meets expectations" with concerns about your level of participation in the group.

4. The company moves mid-level managers to cubicles and creates far more open space for employees to convene. Executives with offices are gone 90 percent of the time and no one uses the open space areas.

5. And at home, on top of career changes, you may experience a house move, new baby, new relationship, divorce, child off to college, loss of significant other's job, property damage, stock market dive, and on and on.

I recognize that some of these might not seem crazy to you. You might even recall being in the lead of one such example. But your view is through your lens. If you made the decision, you likely had more data than most others and have a reason and perspective for the change. Even if so, remember that each person has one lens through which to view the world.

Unravel the Complexity

Most situations that feel crazy are far more complex than you might initially think. In almost any situation, a good first action is to lay out, with specificity, what is happening. That picture of what you know will help you get some distance, see what you don't know, and generate insights for understanding and action.

The world is complex and fragile. Rarely do leaders see that they are creating crazy.

24

Liliana had a pattern of intervening in her team's development of strategies. She was a brilliant strategist, far smarter than anyone on her team at the time. The crazy-making part was her tendency to set a broad expectation, jump in to collaborate when the work was not as expected, and then criticize the team's lack of ability and creativity. The team became disenfranchised and turned over the creativity to Liliana, reinforcing her earlier judgment. Working with the team, I had them lay out the sequence of events, what happened, what was said, and what happened then. The team isolated opportunities to engage early on with Liliana, establishing a new way to actively use their boss's thinking. Liliana was then happy to share the credit for the team's remarkable result as the work reflected some of her ideas and interests. She began to see the brilliance in the team—a win-win once the team stopped resisting Liliana's way of working.

Focusing on facts reduces anxiety and helps to unravel the complexity. With the facts in a diagram, the team could actually see that they needed to engage their boss differently to both enhance their ideas and reduce their pain. The facts could just as easily have shown little opportunity to act as well.

Dive into the data and then look through different lenses to expand your thinking about the situation or person. Consider how different people, departments, organizations, and countries see the situation, problem, solution, or opportunity. There are always multiple lenses with valid ways of seeing. It is possible they might see your perspective as a bit crazy too.

Find a Path for Action

Sometimes you simply need to find a possible path for action. You might decide to work with the craziness, using one of your strengths to meet the challenge of crazy. You might see that the action needs to be initiated by someone else. In crazy situations, we can learn from taking the actions that are possible—to learn and find new lines of action. Here's an example of embracing reality to find a path forward:

> *A clinical development team was briefing me on their recent history. The project was initiated with the company's acquisition of an asset. In the business development process, that asset was clearly not fully vetted, yet leadership expected the program to succeed, and enthusiastically put it into their pipeline. Liam, the team leader who was assigned post-acquisition, was surprised by the significant scientific challenges, uncovering more each day. The political reality was that no one could address the problem with senior leaders. Those leaders had driven the initial acquisition decision and would not want to*

shoulder the accountability (or blame). Not only was the return on investment in jeopardy, but some team members resented investing their career time on a low-value project. Liam was experienced, had good relationships with senior leaders, and was able to pivot and focus on reality rather than complain or resist. He created a best-case outcome and developed team alignment on the focus and plan. The team found a meaningful path forward. They delivered the outcome with excellence and pride.

In this case, the organization made a mistake; they were not intending to acquire an asset that proved challenging. The leader and team had to transcend their emotional resistance.

We all feel better when we are in active mode, but with craziness afoot, move carefully and intentionally.

Have Good Boundaries

Guard against letting a crazy scenario or person consume your time and energy. In all likelihood, the craziness has nothing to do with you. In most cases, your boundary-setting rests in the level of investment you make. Consider this:

An organization made a big, public commitment to innovation, yet everyone knew that the culture was highly risk averse. The launch was full of training and buttons and balloons. Some people participated in the webinars, others did not. Some tried to use the initiative to bolster innovation activities already underway on their team. In six months, nothing was being said about innovation. The balloons had long since burst.

When your resistance is to a person, boundaries can be an important mechanism to maintain sanity. Maybe the person tugs on your wiring with an aggressive criticism or is chaotic in their work process, with changes at every turn. I tell clients to think about putting a "bubble of protection" around themselves and focus on the work. What does the imaginary bubble do? It can protect you from your own emotions. You have to change the way you allow the reality to affect you.

Having good boundaries doesn't mean that you withdraw from the craziness. Rather, you identify the risks and rewards and keep finding a solid ground from which to act. When all else fails, you can adjust to or accept the reality—the craziness may simply be the context for the world in which you are choosing to create.

～

And then, there are families—all a bit crazy. I will leave it at that. Even in families, we often resist what has been going on for decades, rather than embrace our crazy family dynamics.

From small to big, local to global, organization to organization, family to family, the world can appear to be, and is, a bit crazy. Embrace that *people are funny* and *the world is crazy* in order to bring new or renewed energy to your creating.

> "*Most people treat the present moment as if it were an obstacle that they need to overcome. Since the present moment is life itself, it is an insane way to live.*"
> *Eckhart Tolle, Teacher and author of*
> *The Power of Now and A New Earth*

Start Your Thinking

1. When your emotions start to churn or boil, lay out the facts and what patterns of action or behavior you see.
2. What pattern of thinking or behavior of yours is in conflict with this reality?
3. Can you isolate a new point of interaction?
4. If not, can you create a bubble to protect yourself from your own emotions?

Use the Drawing Board in the Possibility Thinker Tools™ to give you the crazy world you are seeing.

*Remarkable results unfold over time
and sometimes land in a different
shape than imagined.*

4. Allow The Future To Evolve

I t would be lovely and exciting if our clear intention and hard work would ensure our desired outcome. But the world is crazy; and a truly remarkable result always evolves over time.

Remarkable Is Not Predictable

As asserted before, we are not in control of much at all other than our own thinking and behaviors (and sometimes not even that).

I am always amused to hear what people think they or others have control over. So often, someone in marketing or research will say that at least salespeople have control over their results. However, sales targets are based on data, opinions, and desire. They are driven by people who can take action and have influence, but no control over the

31

customer. Confident sales leaders and representatives who reach for the remarkable know that the outcomes are uncertain. We can plan, pivot, and persevere—but any result that would be remarkable is not predictable. That doesn't mean it's random; rather remarkable is embedded with uncertainty of the final outcome and path.

Allowing Is A Mindset

When I have taken the time to set very clear intended outcomes, one of my biggest challenges is to *allow the results to unfold.* That means that you as the creator—

1. Can hold in the same hand your desire for the outcome and the uncertainty of realization.
2. Step out of your "driver" role and lift yourself up to see past, present, and future alternatives.
3. Don't give up, but use reality to inform the plan or reshape the specifics of your result.

In your thinking, you are open to see anew.

Consider how this leader, in his first big role, allowed his vision to unfold:

> *Tom was a young, new leader in the organization with three hundred people in his group. He was given a charter for innovative change, both in talent and impact—big impact for the organization. He knew exactly what he wanted*

32

to create and saw the path forward. He put together a very clear desired end-state and the plan to execute. When he made his proposal, the very same leadership group who set the expectation for him told him that he was going too far in his thinking. Tom was disheartened, to put it mildly. After the anger subsided, Tom developed a longer-term plan with some clear milestones that would appeal to his co-creators. Then, he took the next steps, building his team's capability and belief that they could execute. He simply started delivering smaller outcomes toward his bigger picture. And he got to know the leaders and what they cared about, not to mention the crazy dynamics among the senior leaders. Tom's periodic updates helped the senior leaders build confidence in Tom. Two years later, Tom found himself on a much bigger stage, having demonstrated his ability and commitment that would challenge leadership to take the plunge into what they actually wanted to accomplish all along. Five years later, Tom is in the lead on the very same innovation across his industry.

High achievers have a particularly difficult time easing into the culture of decision-making, the unspoken anxiety and competition among senior people, and finding a way to weave their results into a new reality.

Get Up Above the Battlefield

In sports, owners covet a "game-time coach" who can adapt to unexpected contingencies on the field. In the military, a war-time general whose "perfect plan" unravels after one battle achieves victory only if the leader can visualize the potential movement of troops.

Think of the path to your remarkable results as a series of battles. When you are experiencing resistance, challenges, and barriers, it is time to "get above the battlefield" to see the whole, i.e., all the people and plans in action. When the work is going particularly well, you also might want to get above the battlefield to assess where you are and what alternatives lie ahead. That may reveal some aspect or barrier you could not have imagined that makes the intended outcome impossible. In those times, you might find an even better outcome beginning to unfold. In the artist's world, this unexpected positive result is called a "happy accident." The artist has a vision for the painting, gets started, and at some point, a few brushstrokes show some unexpected beauty.

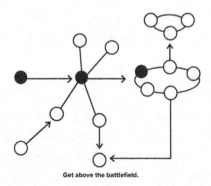

Get above the battlefield.

34

You may decide that the time is not right for your remarkable result as imagined. You may slow the action down or put the work aside intentionally. It's often only in hindsight that a desired creation put aside can emerge as an even better or revised idea at the right time.

⤶

Setting your sights and then elevating your view from time to time can loosen your grip on having your original idea come into being. Embrace the creative process at the same time that you drive toward your goal.

> *"You have to take risks. We will only understand the miracle of life fully when we allow the unexpected to happen."*
>
> *Paulo Coelho, Author*

Start Your Thinking

1. Are you aware when you're pushing rather than allowing a result?
2. When you hit a roadblock, draw a picture of the "battlefield" to understand and have ideas *and* to see whether you need to rest for a while.
3. As you look over the battlefield, do you see any new possibilities, perhaps better than your goal?

Use the Drawing Board in our Possibility Thinker Tools™ to lay out the reality you see.

35

CREATION

What better way to live than bringing important ideas into reality? What are you most committed to creating right now?

---

5. Everything Starts With An Idea

Every result, relationship, or conversation, whether planned or simply observed, is brought into existence by someone's thought. By definition, an idea is a "thought or conception that potentially or actually exists in the mind as a product of mental activity."

All the great inventions started with an idea. In some cases, the idea was a hypothesis and in others a real intent to solve a problem or create something new.

Big outcomes always start with a big idea:

1. Thomas Edison didn't invent the light bulb, but he did create the first commercially viable one.
2. On May 25, 1961, President John F. Kennedy declared that the US would send a man to the

moon and return him safely back to earth by the end of the decade. Apollo 11 landed on July 20, 1969, seven months before the decade's end.

3. Elon Musk first described his idea to send high-speed passenger pods through a tube in 2013. The test tunnel in Hawthorne is complete. Three "loops" are in planning. Stay tuned!

Do you stimulate your ideas and nurture them into a remarkable result for the future?

Start with Crazy and Work Backwards

In this context, crazy means "with high enthusiasm" or essentially crazy-good. Your remarkable result should unleash desire and ignite your thinking about what is possible. I grabbed the subheading from the following story of remarkable:

"Start with crazy" was Scott Borchetta's mantra. As CEO of The Big Machine Label Group, he and his team created Taylor Swift's successful launch and path to stardom. Early on in the development of the label, Borchetta and his team had thirteen artists and asked themselves the question "What's the craziest thing we can do?" They made up the idea that one of their artists, Taylor Swift, could be the biggest artist in the world. The talent was there. And more importantly, there

was tremendous and sustained hard work on the team's and Taylor Swift's parts. I love their quote that "when you invite crazy into the room, crazy becomes reality." So, start with crazy, whatever that means to you.

Did you ever get a big (maybe even crazy) idea and immediately start to make it smaller? Or, have you questioned or reshaped the idea to be more to your boss's liking or (worse) to be more *realistic*? Big ideas can be scary—what if you declare your intention and cannot deliver? Scott Borchetta candidly revealed that his team's crazy idea generated a *motivating fear of failure*, saying that he "believes we have always done our best work when everything is on the line." You don't have to have everything on the line, but I'm encouraging you to create your heart's desire even if it's scary.

Some of the crazy ideas I've supported with my clients include:

1. Changing the way drugs are developed.
2. Becoming a "magnet" for talent, not only attracting high-potentials into the group but embracing that top talent will also move on to other opportunities.
3. Transforming a service practice into a strategic problem-solving practice.
4. Returning to profitability in two years after thirteen years of huge losses.

41

Your crazy ideas do not need to be communicated from the start. I often encourage keeping the crazy in your back pocket so that you don't scare the wrong people.

The Hardest Question: What Do I Want?

Whether you are considering a career move, a major initiative, a team's strategic vision, or simply the critical meeting this afternoon, often the hardest question you will face is: What do **I WANT**? If you ask that question right now, does your brain freeze? Do you think, it's not about me and my desire, it's about the business or job? Do you shy away from doing the work to determine what you most want to create? I do all of those unless I remember to make myself, my life, and my work very important to me.

When you can combine your idea with a strong emotional desire, you put a different kind of energy to the work. You will be far more compelling with co-creators. You will persevere when key challenges or naysayers become obstacles. I ask teams that develop a shared vision of their desired future, "How much do you truly *want* this possibility?"

Sometimes you can use knowing what you don't want to crystallize your idea of what you do want. When I talk to people about their career objectives, they often are clearer about what they don't want.

1. *"I want a boss who isn't authoritarian."* So, what kind of boss do you want?

2. *"I want a job that doesn't limit my growth."* So, what are your capabilities and experience that you want to extend into a future job?

3. *"I want a company that doesn't put my life out of balance."* So, what exactly does balance look like in your ideal job and life?

When I ask the follow-on question, I often get the deer-in-the-headlights look. That's okay, just dig in and think through what you truly want.

Your desired result can also change over time. Your work-life situation may have shifted. Your resources and talent may have changed. For example:

Writing a book has been on my life timeline for twenty-five years. In 2008, I started a blog to find my voice and develop my thinking. Over the years, I have revised my idea of what I want from a published book. In my thirties, I had a clear vision of being on the Oprah show, creating fame and fortune. However, at this stage in my career, I now want two outcomes: 1) a legacy to leave with my clients, friends, son, and grandchildren and 2) to extend my reach to an emerging generation of leaders. I had to ask myself what is most important to me and what I am willing to do to fill the big gaps in my marketing "platform," which is required for most big books. With that intention, I will

*allow the future value and extension of this
book to unfold naturally.*

Allow Time for Your Thinking

Most people are comfortable being in action, often
skipping the work of critical thinking. Every leadership
team I've worked with breathed a sigh of relief when it
moved from envisioning the future to planning actions.
Project teams often default to a smart or controlling
leader or governance body. It's easy to move quickly
to action once a seemingly good, logical idea has been
formed.

For truly remarkable results, allow your ideas to
flow and "pop" into something exciting and inspiring—
again considering *exactly* what you want. Think like a
designer or artist who puts pencil to paper or paint down
on canvas. The artist steps back to see the effect, then
moves in close to consider "How does this look? Is this
what I want?"

Use your co-creators to challenge and enrich
your idea.

1. Who in your network would supportively challenge your thinking?
2. Who are the smartest, most creative people you
   know?
3. Whose thinking must you integrate with your
   idea to move ahead?

Co-creators are the people with whom you need to partner, collaborate, and engage so they endorse your idea or targeted result.

There may be co-creators who should not be involved until an idea is further developed. Don't be shy; rather, be intentional about who you engage in your idea generation. The ultimate idea is still your own. Listen with an ear for what would "thrill you to create."

Sometimes your best thinking comes about when staring at the wall or the ocean. Allow the best idea to emerge without mentally strenuous effort. I often have had remarkable ideas when on vacation. My mind slows down and nature or a new city distracts and enriches my thinking. And when not on vacation, I often grab a notepad to draw ideas or literally sit in a peaceful spot to let my mind de-focus and wander. I put the pad away and come back the next day to see what I saw earlier.

After you have exhausted your thinking, step back for a while and then return to ask: "Is this what I want?" and "If not this, then what?"

Remarkable Results Are Not Only Big Ideas

Smaller, simpler ideas might be exactly what is needed. When you hear remarkable, you think the outcome must be big. Or you have a boss who wants big thinking regardless of the situation.

Remarkable results are *exactly what you want to create*. You may want the project to be completed on time and within budget. While a stretch, it's not going to become front-page news. Or you may want to establish a trusted relationship with a partner. Those results might not be so BIG, but they are indeed what you want to target. You may find as you get more specific on these smaller ideas, that there is plenty of room to create remarkable.

Smaller results can start with an idea to create an experience. At work, small results might be an outcome from a team meeting or conversation. You might want a new beginning with a key relationship or the experience of enthusiasm for the plan ahead. In your personal life that experience might be a birthday party, a walk in the woods, a fishing trip, or a wide-ranging conversation with a friend. Again, the magic is in taking the little bit of time to really think about what you want to create in those experiences.

In fact, all big results require many small results along the way. So, once you have your ultimate idea, the work is in creating it through smaller, immediate results.

⤺

Right now, I am creating in many parts of my life. Here are some of the ideas on my storyboard:

1. The last decade (or two) in my career so that I leave a strong legacy with my clients and their networks.

2. A virtual practice focused on the middle layer of leaders in an organization so that I contribute to the next generation.
3. An oil painting hobby that loosens my creativity and builds my confidence as an artist.
4. Deeper relationships with all my family and friends, who are and will be closest to my spirit.

To springboard into your most important ideas, start with thoughts that are both crazy *and* exactly what you want.

> *"If I have a thousand ideas and only one turns out to be good, I am satisfied."*
> *Alfred Nobel, Swedish inventor with 355 patents*

Start Your Thinking

1. What ideas have you put aside because you don't have the authority to decide or execute?
2. What outcome could be remarkable if you did the thinking now?
3. What do you most want in your work? Career? Life?

Start by imagining "exactly what you want."

6. Almost Anything Is Possible

What is possible? How will you know if your idea is possible or not? If you start with a crazy-good idea, it will always seem a bit impossible.

Walk through your day and see all the amazing creations that are taken for granted. The ones you would say are "impossible" if asked to endorse them now. Trains, planes, and automobiles. Radios, microwaves, and televisions. The personal computer, cell phones, and the internet. The pyramids, the Great Wall of China, and Mount Rushmore. The creators started their thinking with an idea and sustained the energy to keep working it into reality.

The question is: Are you willing to find out whether your desired remarkable result is possible? Or will you modify your desire based on what others think is possible? How do others know what is possible?

Guard Against Your Reasonableness

I am not a fan of SMART goal-setting, which many organizations use in their performance planning. SMART stands for Specific, Measurable, Attainable, Relevant, and Time-Bound. It's specifically, exclusively, the "attainable" element that hangs me up.

Here's my reason: making a goal attainable too often means the individual or team backs away from what might be remarkable. In my thinking, if you get very clear about what your end-state looks like, you will cover specific, measurable, and time-bound. Relevant seems like a no-brainer; how many teams create a goal that is irrelevant to their charter? It's the attainable element that feeds on our human desire to make sure that we are successful. Using the "is this goal reasonable?" filter usually kills any aspect that is special or remarkable about the outcome. So, even if your company uses a SMART system, tuck the remarkable in your pocket.

For example, the team that targeted changing the way drugs were made at their company didn't write that down on their charter or in their performance goals. They kept the goal in the background of the work underway, looking for opportunities or relationships that would benefit their ultimate remarkable result.

To be clear, I am not saying don't use SMART goals or your company's framework. I am saying that you can create beyond the guidelines and systems embedded in your organization.

Optimism Is a Choice that Requires Energy

Optimism is defined as a hopefulness and confidence in the future success of desired outcomes. It's an attitude, a way of thinking. It's a choice you can make. But, it requires sustained energy.

What stands in the way of our natural enthusiasm for what does not easily look possible? There are at least four common barriers.

1. **Physical boundaries**—For many of the creations at the beginning of this chapter, there were clear physical or scientific barriers. Those barriers had to be turned into problems to solve in order to create the ultimate outcome. Don't give up on your idea—solve the problem.

2. **Lack of authority**—Some ideas require approval by an individual or a governing body. When you do not have the authority to act, you have to imagine the pathway to engage those who do. Find the authority you need and never discount your personal power.

3. **Lack of resources**—Many people and organizations can conceive of an outcome that simply costs more than they have in financial and talent resources. An optimistic question might be: "Who does or will have the resources?" Or, "Can we do things differently?

4. **Fear**—Often before you ever share an idea, you get stopped by your own lack of confidence or commitment. Or, as you are moving ahead, you lose steam and find that fear of failure or success is at the core of the perceived barrier. Identifying the fear as an internal conversation is a critical start. Then revisit your original desire for the outcome. Maybe the fear is informing you. Maybe you just need to keep moving.

When faced with barriers, it is very easy to step back from your brilliant idea or to prematurely accommodate the thinking that challenges it. Don't do it. Refuel your energy by talking with co-creators, reviewing your successes, or simply putting your head down to do the next set of tasks.

> *Remarkable results are always highly uncertain and require deliberate action to see what is possible.*

Make Naysayers Useful

Do you wish people in your work and life would get on board with your biggest ideas or those that require meaningful change? The bigger, the crazier, or the more different the idea, the more naysayers it will attract. That's a fact. Even if your idea would solve the biggest current problem. Even if everyone would agree that they want your remarkable result.

You will always have naysayers. A naysayer is someone who is critical of, objects to, or opposes your idea.

If you don't have any naysayers, I would question whether you have set out for something truly remarkable. In fact, you might consider naysayers as crucial to your success. They validate that you are onto something big. If a serious naysayer is also a co-creator (i.e., someone you need to come along on the journey), then you must listen to that person with a very open ear. In fact, high impact and creativity rarely occur without co-creators who start with disparate views and find an ultimate synergy of ideas.

Naysayers are great resources to hear how they think about your intention, the barriers to success, and the requirements. In fact, sometimes the best ideas come from vehement disagreement or widely differing ideas. Rather than resist naysayers, use their objections in a positive way—to learn about the work ahead of you and the people who matter.

Understand and Include Slow-Downers

I am sure you have encountered people who essentially slow down the movement forward. People who want or need to be informed or involved (even though they don't really have a role at all). Someone who intercedes in the decision, even when lacking authority in the matter. Before trying to blast through a slow-downer (especially ones with power), consider incorporating them into the communication loop, and consider what really matters to them (and whether you can provide some of that). In fact, the slow-downer might just want to be relevant to you and the remarkable result you have underway.

Impossibility Arrives Through Experience

Only your creative experience can tell you if something is impossible. Even if someone else has attempted a similar or the same outcome, you will never know whether you can succeed until you put in the time and energy.

When an idea seems overly challenged, ask yourself:

1. What do you need to find out before you put the idea on the shelf?
2. Are you actually in the way of this idea for which you have a deep desire (e.g., unwilling to take risks, insufficient time, wavering desire, etc.)?

You *can* find that some ideas are in fact impossible (right now or maybe forever). Any single or combination of the barriers above may tip your idea into the impossible category. That's okay. Just don't classify your idea as impossible without careful thought and discovery.

⌇

I find it most useful to think that (almost) anything is possible. You never know how ideas might percolate or unfold over time with the right work and perseverance.

> "The best scientist is open to experience and begins with romance—the idea that anything is possible."
> *Ray Bradbury, Author and screenwriter*

Start Your Thinking

1. What "wiring" do you have about setting a goal that others might say is impossible?
2. Can you match your desire to what seems impossible?
3. How would you know if your idea is indeed possible?

Start Your Thinking

A picture makes you think critically and creatively. Your diagram can pull people into a shared vision or stimulate new ideas.

7. A Picture Draws You Into The Future

To create remarkable results, you need the ability to envision the picture of your desired future-state. The word *envision* implies "seeing" the future. Seeing indicates a visual picture. Words are required to *describe* that picture but are not the vision. Another way of thinking about it is that "the devil of creation is in the details." Let's start with a simple example:

> *I want a wonderful family dinner with good food and lively conversation. A crystal-clear picture of that dinner would include who attends, location, table setting, seating arrangement, menu, topics, and dynamics between people. You would need to play the*

movie in your mind to get exactly what you want. Now, this creating might be overkill for most family dinners. But, maybe not if you have a challenging family or Uncle Harry is often difficult or your teenagers answer most questions with "good."

When you have a robust picture in mind, you will carefully plan and see opportunities to act that you might not have seen without your clear, desired picture.

Unpack Your Thinking

So often, ideas and observations are expressed with words. The challenge is that words can mask your meaning or intent. When you imagine what you want to create, big or small, personal or work-related, you may move into action as soon as you have words to capture your intent. But, is there sufficient clarity to get the best start or pull your idea into reality?

Most of us stop far short of a multifaceted picture of our desired future reality. What are all the aspects to your desired end-state? What concrete results (e.g., product, financial, time, quality, etc.) do you envision? And what qualitative results (e.g., relationship, reputation, innovation, etc.)? Start your thinking with a mind map of key aspects.

Clarity will come from "unpacking" what you mean by the words in your idea. When you have identified key aspects to your remarkable result, ask three questions for each aspect until you are clear:

1. What do I mean by _____?
2. What would _____ look like?
3. What do I truly want?

Suppose your remarkable result is to improve customer satisfaction and increase revenues by 25 percent. What do you mean by improve satisfaction? What would that look like—retention and returning customer rates? Would that satisfaction attract new customers—what profile and where? By 25 percent, do you mean global revenues? Do you have a breakdown by region or country in mind?

If your targeted result is an organization dynamic, capability, or cultural element, your task to make your result concrete is even more important and challenging.

You can test your intention by thinking more broadly about the different types of outcomes. Three types of outcomes that are important in any creation:

1. The What you do.
2. The How you do it, and
3. The So What impact.

As you craft your future picture, check your thinking by each type of outcome. Use the "So What?" question to make sure you have gotten to your real intended impact.

For example, you may say you want to grow revenues by 25 percent overall, with a 50 percent increase in emerging markets. So what? If you grew revenues by 25 percent, what would that outcome produce that you don't have now? You can say "so that we have sufficient resources for new product development." Or, "so that we improve investor confidence and continued funding." And of course, if so, what would that look like?

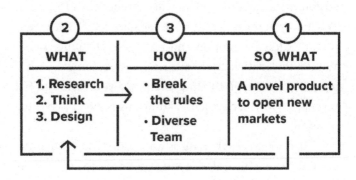

Draw or Diagram to Show Complexities

Whatever you are creating, start by drawing a diagram or picture—literally. When faced with critical, challenging thinking, it is powerful to put your ideas on paper. Draw your idea or information into a diagram or picture that shows or tells the current story. The drawing doesn't have to be elegant; a mind map or timeline might do the trick. The important part is to expand the picture to include all the aspects of your remarkable result.

Why draw or create a diagram? To engage both sides of your brain. The "left" side is typically thought of as the logical/language/reasoning side. The "right" side sees patterns and takes a more holistic/creative view. When you talk about an idea or put an outline together, you're most often using your left side. When you draw a picture or diagram, you're engaging the right side to "see" the data organized in a framework or picture. That picture will allow you to think more critically and creatively inside and outside the frame. See the simple examples below.

A Simple Mind Map

A Timeline

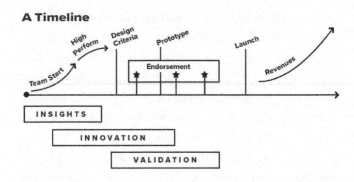

An End-State

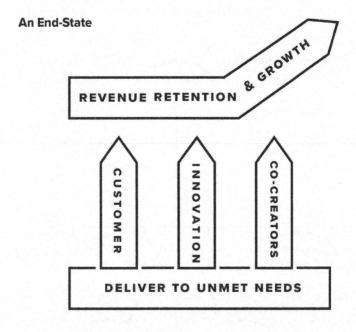

For each of these examples, you would add elements and specificity, building out a more complete and compelling picture of your targeted result. With a picture, you're better able to:

1. Notice what's missing,
2. Generate other ideas,
3. Check your thinking, and
4. More easily include others in your thinking.

Some people are very visual. On many teams, there is one person who jumps to the whiteboard to lay out a conceptual framework or organize the discussion. If that isn't you, you may find it challenging or awkward to draw in order to think. At the very least, draw a bubble chart of elements and/or a timeline or flowchart to help you think.

If you're not convinced yet, ask any design engineer, new product developer, or scientist whether a picture helps them create a better product.

A Picture Creates a Tension Between Now and the Future

The picture of your desired future-state will create a tension between your current reality and the future. The degree of tension is dependent on two things:

1. Your emotional attachment—how much do you want it?
2. The distance or challenge in reaching that future.

If your desire is moderate, the tension will lag. Without enough of a challenge, the tension will not pull as strongly.

When your vision of the future is clear, all that occurs around you can become an opportunity to move the action forward. When the creative tension is taut, it can seem as if the future is pulling you into it.

Jason was frustrated with a senior governance committee comprised of leaders who were top in their field but not very strategic in their business planning. When he started envisioning the critical outcome he wanted to create, he saw that he had to engage with these leaders in their field quite differently. He needed to orchestrate the thinking and decisions across leaders by drawing on their expertise and pulling them into his ideas about where they could take the business. Jason painted the picture in one-on-one discussions and invisibly orchestrated key co-creators' discussions to have them create the tension to pull them forward together. Over several months, Jason was able to chart a new strategic path for which he did not get "credit." What he got was full senior co-creator commitment to their shared intent. That commitment was a treasure, pulled through by creating the tension between current state and the future.

Very smart people may dismiss this practice because they are very good at processing data in their big brains. But I have never worked with a brilliant person who, if agreeable, doesn't see new things from their drawing (although I am often doing the drawing at their direction).

～

Painting the picture takes some time but can be done in many sittings or as a team. You can only be clear about what you can be clear about. Getting really clear is very hard work, and sometimes we can't get quite clear. Your picture may get clearer over time. But, don't let the uncertainty of the future stop you from putting a stake in the ground. You can always pull the stake up and move it three feet.

Practice on important creations, or at least ask your team to paint the picture—and push for real value.

"I've always been amazed by Da Vinci, because he worked out science on his own. He would work by drawing things and writing down his ideas. Of course, he designed all sorts of flying machines way before you could actually build something like that."

Bill Gates, entrepreneur and philanthropist

Start Your Thinking

1. Can you see your remarkable result in your mind's eye?
1. How can you describe all the elements so that another person can see it exactly the same as you?
3. Put your picture on paper so that you can think and see it even more clearly.

Use the What-How-So What and the Drawing Board tools in Possibility Thinker Tools™.

CHALLENGES

Behind our personal lens we have all of our history, thinking, beliefs. We look at each and every situation and person through that lens without realizing we are making decisions and seeing data.

8. We Each Look Through A Unique Lens

To be most successful in your work and life, you have to start with understanding your own wiring, which offers a unique lens on the world.

We Are a Product of Our Human "Being"

You are a product of your personal biology, history, and environment. You can recall your earliest memory. You know your biological or adopted parents and your family history; and, you may know about your family genetics, maybe even your IQ. You can remember schools you went to, books you read, teachers you liked, and those you didn't. You have stories about how you had fun, what you excelled at, and of what you are most proud. You can rattle off why you chose the schools you attended. You can recite your resume and point to managers, colleagues, and companies you most appreciated. You might have recurring frustrations, a failure or two, and maybe a traumatic life experience. You also have private thoughts about your greatest pleasures and fears. Think about the innumerable instances that are logged into your memory and linked together, some conscious and others hidden. All of these data points create your lens on life and that lens shapes:

1. Your values and beliefs,
2. What you see and what you don't,
3. How you think,
4. Who you engage and trust, and
5. What ideas capture your heart and mind.

You can't change the past, but you can examine and be aware of how that medley of experiences could help or hinder how you behave and where you spend your time. When you succeed, you do so in large part because of your history. And, when you make mistakes or fail, the cause may be rooted in your history too.

Our Lens Shapes What We See

You look through your lens every moment of the day without awareness that it colors your perspective. You may have heard the phrase "looking through rose-colored glasses" to refer to someone who sees the world in a positive way. Better to say that I look through the "Mary Mavis glasses" at each and every person and situation. I see each in my own unique way—different from anyone else.

In fact, your historical lens will filter what you see and what you don't see in any given situation. Suppose we both participate in a meeting. You might see the team leader late to the meeting; I see the meeting starting at the usual ten minutes after the hour. You see Sara raise her eyebrows when Sam makes a proposal; my focus is on the leader who is positively engaged with Sam. We all know we think differently, but we often don't realize that we never have the same observations. Then we debrief the meeting with an unconscious assumption that we are all starting from the same data set. And, we never have all the data!

The Mary Mavis "glasses prescription" can change not just with different data and personal history. It can adjust over time and with feelings and moods.

Your Unique Wiring Moves You to Decisions

Not only do you see a select set of data through your lens, you process that data through your historical database. Over time your lens and patterns of experience develop what I call your "wiring"—your automatic response to new situations.

Wiring can support or drive your success. It can also be the stumbling block or blind spot. Often the same wiring is both a positive and negative driver. For example, if a leader is wired to win, to not only meet but exceed all expectations, that wiring will help her sustain the effort, think creatively, or do whatever the result requires. At the same time, that leader might jeopardize the team's confidence with harsh criticism or knowingly or unconsciously refrain from collaboration with her peers.

When I am working with someone who has some sticky wiring (i.e., tough to loosen), I like to draw a timeline from birth to present. I ask the leader to lay in situations and people associated with past experiences related to the wiring. We then track how the leader's decisions were made, often from early experiences. I always tell my clients that I am not a psychologist, but that I know a lot about people. Understanding your own wiring and considering what you know about others is a key success factor in life. Here is some actual problematic wiring that my clients have disclosed:

1. "My parents came from nothing. They focused on education, and our dinner table was filled with aggressive debate."
2. "When challenged, I tend to 'go into the ravine' to fight my opponent as I did in my boyhood."
3. "I learned to do what I was told to avoid the chaos in my family."
4. "Everyone was counting on me in my family; I took on the role of 'fixer.'"

5. "Winning was everything to my father; failure was not acceptable, let alone mistakes."

Wiring doesn't have to originate in your family. You can easily have had work and mentor experiences that strongly shaped your automatic responses. Wiring also doesn't have to be your hidden challenges. It can be your way of thinking that has been central to your success. Whether supportive or problematic, when you can pull the thread through your timeline from childhood to now, you know you have identified very strong wiring.

Many years ago, a wonderful colleague of mine left a voice mail following a client meeting. I listened to the first sentence: "Mary, I have some feedback for you." In our firm, we took giving and welcoming feedback very seriously. But that day I had an emotional reaction and hung up the phone. Twelve hours later, I listened to the full voice mail, which continued from that first sentence with "You did an amazing job facilitating the client meeting today. Your facilitation made a huge difference in the dialogue..." You see, my personal "wiring" is primed for hearing criticism and seeing my own imperfections. With one sentence, I leapt to my underlying assumption that I probably disappointed my colleague. Knowing that about myself, I have learned to ask for feedback,

73

affirming and improvement-oriented, even though my wiring cries its warning. And most importantly, I remind myself that all of that feedback comes through the other person's lens into my lens and wiring.

You may be more or less confident as a person or on a particular topic, but your wiring takes over every time unless you are highly mindful that you are guided by your lens. In many teams, debate of hot topics or decisions can evolve into two or more "camps," and each camp tries to win an argument by staying put and pushing their rationale. Wouldn't it be superb if someone on your team said, "Let's take each perspective and make sure we understand the background of each person's view (i.e., their lens)!"

I don't believe you can dismantle wiring. But, I know you can loosen the wires, understand them better, anticipate and be intentional in button-pushing situations, and sound alarms if problematic wiring hooks you. The question is "Do you want to work with your wiring or not?"

Look across the table, desk, or online meeting today and recognize that each person in the conversation has a unique lens. What an opportunity if you use it as a way to understand and work with them. How interesting if you think about it that way. You, your bosses, your children and loved ones, your neighbors and community members all have unique lenses.

Our complex, often unconscious differences are why working and living with other people can be challenging or delightful.

> *We are shaped by our thoughts; we become what we think.*
>
> *Buddha*

Start Your Thinking

1. For a challenging situation right now, what lens do you use to think about what is happening?
2. In a recent meeting, can you identify the key aspects to each person's lens on a decision?
3. Can you change your lens slightly to make a conversation with a co-creator more effective?

We snap to our opinions about so many things. The more expert we are, the more difficult it can be to realize that our opinions are a product of our lens, not the TRUTH.

9. Opinions Are Not The Truth

We form opinions in a *snap*! When you wake up, you have opinions about how your body feels, how late you might be, and what would taste good for breakfast. You have opinions about the weather, the traffic and drivers, the meetings planned for the day, and your conversation with a friend the previous evening. All of us are *opinion machines.*

Note that I use the word *opinion* as a synonym for assessment and evaluation. All of these words rely on standards, an imperfect data set, and people. Without people, none of these exist (i.e., if a tree falls in the forest with no one around, does it make a sound?).

There Are Facts, and There Are Opinions

Let's face it, facts are just plain boring. That might be why we don't converse by exchanging facts. Opinions charge up the dialogue and convey our point of view, whether strong or open to collaboration. For example, if I tell you that *the world is crazy*, you might disagree with me. You might say *the world is exciting*. Validating opinions requires offering facts that are concrete, behavioral patterns over time, etc. However, the natural way to unravel one's thinking is to justify an opinion with sub-opinions. The world is crazy: too many people are hungry, corporations are corrupt, etc. The world is exciting: science is breaking new ground, technology is forging new experiences like augmented reality, etc. *None of these are facts!* It's not until you have the data set that you even know if you agree. And your agreement would be your *opinion* also, not a *fact*.

Your opinions are based on all of the elements that make up your unique lens on life and any standards that your communities, organizations, and families have about the matter at hand. When challenged or just plain thoughtful, you can match your facts to your standards to state a grounded opinion.

A grounded opinion is based on a reasonable set of data against clear expectations. Clear expectations are stated as the desired facts and observations, not general descriptions. To be truly compelling, you can unfold what you mean. For example:

"Great leaders like Roger create loyal followers."

1. To me, "great" is a leader who creates remarkable, sustainable results over decades.
2. "Loyal followers" are those willing to act and to challenge that leader over the time they are engaged.
3. My experience and observations bring me to the conclusion that Roger is a great leader.

Okay, so you aren't going to actually talk that way, but you get the idea. Shared expectations are developed through dialogue. Once shared, the words can be a shortcut to clear feedback and understanding.

Even with clear expectations and a large data set, opinions are NOT the Truth (with a capital T) about any person, place, or situation. All you would need to do is:

1. Change the expectations,
2. Use a very different lens on the subject, or
3. Expand, shrink, or change the set of data.

If you did any or all of the above, you would have a moderately to extremely different opinion. Think about the way scientists and experts have changed their opinions (e.g., the world is round, etc.).

We Never Have All the Facts

There are very few situations for which we can ever have all the facts. As I mentioned, you select the facts you see based on your lens—as do others. Even if someone shares their facts as true facts—boring as they are—one can never be sure of what is missing. I emphasize this point because your brain will pretend that you have most if not all of the relevant facts all the time. Beware! Pretending you have all of the facts will get you in trouble. When you disagree, don't understand something, or have a strong competing opinion, it's always best to start with a genuine question about the other person's opinion. When you want to advocate for your opinion, work through the facts that are behind it and identify the facts that are missing.

Expert Opinions Hold More Weight

When you have significant experience or expertise, you likely will be even more committed to your opinion. And frankly, the expert opinion in any domain should count more. The boss's opinion (even if wrong) always counts more. The customer's opinion counts more. By *more*, I mean that we need to listen and probe before challenging or dismissing the opinion. Basically, *recognized* expertise, experience or authority should and does add weight to an opinion.

Smart, confident people can derive a strong opinion with limited data or expertise. That opinion coupled with an emotional intent or fear of consequences can lead someone to be blind and deaf to the experts. Since I assume you are smart and confident, you are particularly vulnerable to closing yourself off to differing opinions and the facts that support them.

Human beings don't think this way, so the best you can do is to step back and reflect when your opinion is dismissed, or you immediately feel challenged by another's statement. Ask: "What are the competing and complementary lenses on the matter?" The bottom line is that whatever words you use, they are never the Truth.

And sometimes opinions are expressed for hidden motives—in competition, to gain status, or to block some decision or action. The more power the person has, the greater the impact they have in gaining agreement on their opinion. You have to put your thinking into action to consider the funny person, their lens, and the possibilities for your own actions.

Shared Opinions Can Be Powerful

People can and do agree in their opinions. They can and do make decisions based on a shared opinion. In fact, agreement makes a strongly experienced opinion seem "right." Consider the following:

1. A leadership team that has a shared view of the opportunities in the marketplace.
2. The old-guard employees in a department are skeptical about the announced change.
3. A new, young leader has galvanized her peers in an approach to solve the team's top problem.
4. A strong culture (i.e., how we do things) is a shared opinion that can be positive or destructive.

81

Agreement is good when it is informed, driven by positive intent, tested from different lenses, and put into action.

⬗

Liberate yourself by embracing that you don't have all the data, that your expectations and standards may not be clear, and your opinions can be a starting point for deeper understanding and innovation.

> *"For having lived long, I have experienced many instances of being obliged, by better information or fuller consideration, to change opinions, even on important subjects, which I once thought right but found to be otherwise."*
> *Benjamin Franklin*

Start Your Thinking

1. Is there any difference between your expert assessment and others' opinions?
2. What assessment do you have that you consider to be true? Make the distinction between your assessment/opinion and the facts that you use to support your point.
3. For someone with whom you disagree on something, can you ask three questions that will uncover their supporting facts?

Check out the Possibility Thinker Tool™ for a framework to develop feedback grounded in facts.

Your life will be much happier if you stop thinking you can make people do what you want. You can't. Each of us decides to act.

---

10. You Can't Make Anyone Do Anything

We want to think that if we are logical in our request, direction, or feedback that a person will do what we suggest. That can be true more often than not. But, not always. Sometimes you'll get agreement, but no action. Even when you have power as the boss or an important co-creator or relationship, the other person can (and does) decide whether or not to do what you ask.

Don't Kid Yourself About Your Authority

You began your understanding of power through your original family and the varying structures, personalities, and dynamics. You moved to school and similarly experienced, adopted, or rejected the structures and power dynamics in that domain. At work and with different bosses and organizational cultures, you determine how you can be successful—how to play. But, no one makes you do anything you don't decide to do.

Good ideas are not always followed; employees are often amazed that their bosses do not act on situations of which they have been made aware. Employees do not always change their behavior when given feedback; managers either get angry or give up. Some real examples include:

1. A senior executive saw a new possibility for fostering a new culture of collaboration rather than the competitive internal environment in place. The CEO agreed with her. The business case was clear. Yet, the CEO did nothing. The executive could lead her group and work to influence her peers but could not make the CEO take the lead.

2. A cross-functional team and its leader were beyond frustrated with one team member's consistent lack of delivery in time for the team to meet its deadlines. The team leader gave feedback. The functional manager reinforced the requirement. The team member either could not or would not do what it took to change his work process.

3. A functional team mustered the courage to give their manager clear feedback about their need

for the manager to attend their team meetings, on time and prepared. They were under tight deadlines, and the work was complicated. The manager agreed but continued to be late or absent.

4. A manager gave a direct report feedback and set a clear expectation to follow the established work plan rather than modify the work underway based on his own preferences. Multiple meetings did not produce a change.

When faced with these types of situations, you must first confirm that your expectations and the impact are clear. Ensure shared understanding and underscore or elevate the consequences of no action. Of course, as you do that, also try to discern whether the other person is interpreting the request differently or holds other or competing interests. Also remember that repetition is key to change unless there is a "fire" to put out.

Early in my consulting and coaching work, I realized that even when a client fully collaborated and agreed with the ultimate vision or end-state, the execution of recommendations was not always certain. Sometimes the client's thinking and decision were altered. Though I now tell clients, "Don't do what I suggest you do," out of a desire for their clear decision, I still secretly hope they will take my strongest recommendations. But, I'm clear about who is in charge of the decision to act.

Inquiry, Agreement, and Honor

What can you do when others exercise their right to decline your request, demand, or expectation?

1. *Inquire into the situation* to ensure you understand what is happening and whether there is shared understanding of your thinking.
2. *Get real, mutual agreement.* There are no valid complaints unless an agreement was breached.
3. *Consider the person's capability* to deliver or whether the necessary resources exist.
4. *Think about what the person cares about* to source ideas for influencing.

When conscious of this principle, you can begin your engagement by honoring every person's freedom to think and act. At the same time, as I have said to my son, "With freedom comes responsibility for consequences."

⤶

Each person in an organization, each customer or client, and each person in your family has the privilege and responsibility to make their own decisions and experience both the positive and the unwanted consequences. Free yourself from the belief that you can make anyone do anything!

> *"Except our own thought, there is nothing absolutely in our power."*
>
> René Descartes, French philosopher

Start Your Thinking

1. Do you do what is asked of you at work? At home?
2. Do you make demanding requests? Do you assume people will say yes and do what you ask?
3. What do you think and do when you don't get what you requested?

When your logical argument does not persuade, think about what you know about where the person or people stand on the matter.

11. Go In The Door Someone Is Already Standing In

Influence is required when you cannot get attention, approval, endorsement, or agreement using your most logical, fact-based presentation or request. With influence, you use your personal power to indirectly create the result you want. That influence may be focused on a person, committee or group, department, or co-creator (e.g., customers, patients, etc.). When you need to use your influence with a particular person, you can look for a way to:

Go in the door in which the person is already standing.

Rather than try to convince the person to stand in your door (e.g., adopt the way you think or support your position on a matter, etc.), get a clear picture of their door. Then plan a way to use your understanding of their door to approach or engage the person, in effect, walking through their door first.

Influence Is Not Persuasion, Not Manipulation

So often, influence is mistaken for persuasion. You may try to sway someone by your logical proposal or your detail-rich accounting of what happened and what was needed. Your frustration mounts when you don't gain agreement. Whether the person you're trying to influence is your boss (with a very specific power dynamic) or someone else who has power, it's remarkable how resistant you can be about just finding the door to walk through. Most of us want people to validate that our logic and ideas are right. Influence is about putting that need aside and finding a way to illuminate shared interests.

Influence is not manipulation. Remember, you can't make anyone do anything they don't want to do. The bigger the impact, the less likely you can be successful with a negative intent to manipulate someone. Influence is about pulling someone through your door by walking first through theirs.

Think Backward Through Their Lens

I often hear about a boss who is elusive yet strong in criticism. For illustration, suppose "Sue" is such a boss. She has achieved major success. Imagine that you and every person close to her business results value her exceptional capability. But you get frustrated with Sue's perceived need to be involved in all key decisions and many less important ones. When breaking down what Sue cares most about, you recognize that she:

1. Expects innovation and creativity in business and customer plans.
2. Drives extreme execution through everything, having amazing personal stamina for doing "whatever it takes."
3. Stops at nothing less than exceptional results, period!

But you want to make decisions sooner, calculating when creativity competes with effective execution. Her creative ideas often land on your team late in the planning process, which puts major pressure on the final execution. Reluctantly, you do have to admit that her ideas are always great.

Find a Common Interest or Commitment

Ultimately, you want to answer two questions to find your pathway to and through Sue's door:

1. What *does* she care about?
2. What *should* she care about (but might not see right now)?

Do you share any of the same concerns? If so, go there first—acknowledge a shared interest. Or, if not shared, consider how you can orient your interest toward her concerns. Can you reframe your intended outcome to link to those concerns? Can you ask a question that demonstrates that connection? How can you wrap your interests around what's important to that person?

Going in the door in which Sue is already standing, you might take one or more of these approaches:

1. Anticipate how to get her creative input earlier in the planning cycle, making the interaction one in which she can build on the team's creative concepts rather than shoot down a final proposal.
2. When late-breaking ideas surface, quickly lay out what will be required for full execution, and explain the impact now versus moving to the next quarter.
3. Link every plan back to key results, illuminating the competing demand for resources (time and money).
4. Match Sue's high energy when creating; at the same time, bring a serious tone to the impact on her ability to deliver her results.

Ultimately, Sue wants to be assured that she will get the results she needs, the hard numbers, *and* the innovation that she associates with success. Everything you do can be positioned within that context. Critical conversations can be planned to get ahead of her need to oversee your team's effectiveness.

Where's the influence? If you see "the door she's standing in" and don't resist (telling yourself "that's not my door"), you're better prepared to get what both you *and* Sue want most. She wants results, as do you. You want your team's process to be efficient. Finding the intersection starts with walking through Sue's door.

We Wish We Didn't Have To Influence

Why can it be hard to step back and influence people more strategically in this way? Some of the personal barriers might include:

1. You don't want to leave your "own door." It's more comfortable to maintain your own logical view or ask for what makes sense to you.
2. You don't know what the person cares about. That reality is a call to action that I covered in earlier chapters. You cannot influence people without knowing what matters to them.
3. Your wiring sets you up with an emotional resistance to a person like Sue. In this case, slowing down and getting out of your own way is a good practice—loosen up *your* wires.

When I work with people on influencing, I often hear this complaint: "WHY do I have to influence?" My answer is always, "You don't have to influence unless you can't get results by presenting and persuading." It's only when you hit roadblocks, or know that the key people will or may resist your proposal or request, that you need to take an influencing approach.

～

The fastest way to success is always to go through the door in which the person is already standing, but without the person knowing that you are entering it.

> "The secret of my influence has always been that it remained secret."
>
> Salvador Dali

Start Your Thinking

1. What decisions or outcomes have the strongest competing perspectives among the most powerful co-creators?
2. What co-creator is most important to influence (so that others will fall in place, etc.)?
3. How are the "doors" the same and also different?

*When you are hooked by some outrage
or fear, remember that most people are
not out to get you.*

12. Very Few People Wake Up And Plot To Be Disruptive

It is easy to feel someone is intentionally making your life difficult. Someone makes an assessment of your work that seems fact-less. Another hijacks your meeting with their own concerns. A team member doesn't deliver, making your own delivery impossible. And on and on.

Why We Think People Are Out to Get Us

It wouldn't be a problem if it was one time or infrequent. It wouldn't be concerning if the behavior didn't affect you directly or impact someone you care about. It wouldn't be a problem if you thought the person was simply too new or inexperienced to know better. It wouldn't be a problem if you thought the behavior was in the ballpark of acceptable. It **is** a problem when a pattern of behavior affects your performance or well-being and triggers your past experience or wiring.

Experiencing such a pattern of behavior likely prompts an emotional reaction. Over time and with increasing incidents, you may move from annoyance to disbelief to upset to anger—sometimes racing right to anger if your wiring gets triggered or the stakes are particularly high. You might set in motion a blockade or retaliation. Or, seemingly more benignly, you participate in gossip. Emotion sets up a reaction to their action. Remember Newton's law, for every action, there is an equal and opposite reaction. While not science, the point is that you *are* going to have a reaction looking through your lens.

Some of the crazy-making situations that seem all too common in organizations include:

1. You secured your boss's approval for a key proposal, but right before the leadership team meeting, he stops in to say that he cannot endorse the proposal after all.
2. A colleague calls to say that the VP of a critical function told her to stop work on your project. This is not the first time this VP has undermined your work.
3. Your team leader has given you an important assignment. When you stopped by a team member's desk, however, you saw that he also is working on the analysis.

4. A VP complains about you to your boss because you gave critical feedback to the VP's direct report. Your intention was squarely to hold the team to high standards and the agreed timeline. Your boss asks you to repair the situation.

Whether verbalized or not, you may consider behavior or patterns as characteristics of the person. You view the person as *that way.* You think they are consciously and willfully working to harm you, your work, or the team.

It's Just Not True (Mostly)

VERY FEW people get up in the morning, put on their coat, and think, "How can I make Mary's day miserable?" or "How can I disrupt the productive work underway?" or "How can I disenfranchise all the people who matter to the result?"

It does happen. There are evil or vengeful people in the world. There are people who don't particularly like you. But it's rare that your colleagues, boss, or others are intentionally trying to harm you or sabotage your results.

Instead people act out of their background, their anxieties, their lens on the world, and how they have learned to be successful. Or, they have seen and been treated the exact same way, and either are unaware of your resistance or its impact of their actions. Or, they are unconscious about how you might feel. Or, they have some life stress going on (e.g., illness, sick child, fear of

97

losing their job, etc.). Again, in a rare case, someone might delight in punishing people the way they were punished, but it's unlikely.

Do a Little Therapy on Yourself

The antidote here is for you to catch your emotions and slow down your reaction so that you can examine your own wiring. You have moved into fear. If you think you are angry, that's probably fear underneath. If you're upset, that's likely fear also. What are you afraid might or might not happen?

Think about what the person is doing or saying, how they are operating, and the *so-what* impact that could be driving that behavior and thinking. Lay out the facts in a quick picture or timeline. What facts are you sure about and what have you heard from others? Take a look through the other person's lens: what might they find important enough to take the actions they did? See if the facts and different logic can calm your emotional reaction.

Then, journey inward and consider how your own wiring might be tripping you up. What patterns in your past are similar to the current situations? Through what "story" about the way the world works are you viewing the current facts? What real impact have you experienced in the past that has been triggered now?

If you slow down, you can weave your thinking into an approach that assumes at least neutral intent and creates an approach to create your desired outcome, build that very relationship, or simply let it go and work on something else.

⌒

It is always fruitful to step back and make a more grounded assessment of the situation and people. Ultimately, you want to find your confidence and move into a more personally powerful stance. Frankly, even if someone is out to get you, your approach will be more effective if you heed the advice above.

> *"Holding on to anger is like grasping a hot coal with the intent of throwing it at someone else; you are the one who gets burned."*
>
> *Buddha*

Start Your Thinking

1. Who do you think means you harm, and on what?
2. What are the facts and patterns of action?
3. How is your personal history and wiring pulling you into fear?
4. How would your energy change if you viewed this situation and the people as important challenges rather than a threat?

Inspiration

INSPIRATION

Don't wait to be empowered by anyone.
You have the power. Build it and use it.

13. You Have More Power Than You Use

There are two kinds of power: positional power and personal power. Each of us has some positional power—the authority to act or decide in our roles at work and in life. Whatever your role status, you have the power to fulfill that role well and to make decisions, big or small. You also have a second kind of power—personal power that comes from your trusted relationships, reputation, and influencing ability.

We Rely Most On Positional Power

Most people focus on positional power. What authority do you have, and what decisions can you and your team actually make? Some people use their positional power and some people don't. That might seem odd, but think about it. Can you remember a time when you were begging for someone to finally decide on something?

In most organizations, the roles are defined in job descriptions and the decision authority is defined in governance presentations. Both documents are usually written in general terms, only to find that the reality of who does what and decides what is far more situational and personally driven. And while never stated as such, organizations often unconsciously (or consciously) keep that positional authority loose. Why? Wouldn't it be better if authority were clear? Maybe. It certainly makes sense to most people—especially those people who are not as aware of their personal power. If attempted, the work of getting clear on authority is very challenging. Imagine if you had to live with your entire extended family and broker all the roles and authority from toddlers to teenagers to the elders!

Recognize, Develop, and Use Your Personal Power

The highest-value power is personal power—*the power in you*, not your role. Often when I have worked with a client about a frustrating situation or person, at some point we recognize that the client has more power than they are using. That personal power might be:

1. An ability to "see" the underlying problem and a range of solutions that few others see.
2. An understanding of the other person's concerns and interests and the dynamics among key people.

3. An apolitical nature—no one would imagine a hidden agenda—so he's all about the results.
4. A trustworthy reputation among colleagues that allows for influence or inspires loyalty.

Once beyond frustration, you can use that power with a positive and clear intention and an ability and opportunity to act or initiate others' actions.

There are as many examples of this opportunity as there are organizations, people, and situations. Here are a few to get you thinking:

1. **A leader who is frustrated with ongoing resistance to an organizational change**. She uses her personal power to paint a crystal-clear picture of what the change is and why the change is important to all. She is known for an attitude of no turning back, doing whatever it takes for years. She has fostered deep respect from all with whom she has worked. Given that personal power, she has the ability to be far more demanding of the people involved and can draw them into the change underway.

2. **A technical leader has the charter to achieve a big outcome**. However, the resources are tied up in approvals from other functions. The leader has made the business case multiple times. Then, the leader realizes her personal power in an external reputation with funding partners.

The goal is unattainable without her. She begins to think about how to shift her "case" with a particularly challenging person involved.

3. **A senior leader sees the organization dynamics that are in the way of the leadership group**. The leader also knows what is needed to execute on the strategy. Not until he has a key committee role does the leader see his influence emerging. Now, the leader looks for opportunities for influence with the right people.

Note that I am using the term "leader" to include different *types* of leaders, not *levels*. Each person in an organization can be a leader among peers and colleagues if they decide to think of themselves as powerful.

One caveat: the highest finesse is in wielding one's power without appearing to do so. In the three examples above, you might say "of course," and why didn't the leader just "spell it out"? But often that direct approach causes unnecessary resistance.

⤿

Personal power arises out of who you are and what you accomplish. Use your power strategically and consciously. Think about the outcome for which you are most concerned. What frustrates you or worries you about its achievement? What personal power might you have that you haven't used so far? Give yourself permission to be powerful.

> *"Power is given only to those who dare to lower themselves and pick it up. Only one thing matters, one thing; to be able to dare!"*
>
> *Fyodor Dostoevsky, Russian author*

Start Your Thinking

1. Do you want to have more power in creating remarkable results?
2. What positional power do you have now?
3. How do you have or want to have a personal power with people in your work and life?

Onward

This book is about you. I truly hope that some combination of these chapters has captured your heart and mind and fueled your energy for creating remarkable results.

What result can you now start to imagine that would be remarkable when you bring it into reality?

How are you seeing the interesting work ahead in understanding your co-creators and using that understanding?

What experience would you have in your work and life if you adopted a small set of these concepts and used them pervasively in your world?

In closing, I can honestly say that I consider YOU the remarkable part of my work!

How We Can Work Together?

As I launch this book, I will have several ways for you to continue your journey with me.

1. Read my blog, Monday Morning, by signing up on my website,
2. Listen to upcoming podcasts,
3. Contact me about working with your team(s).

Go now to www.maviscompany.com and download my Possibility Thinker Tools™.

The Possibility Thinker Tools are intended to deepen your understanding and generate new ideas and insights so that you can achieve a truly remarkable result. You can download the tools at www.maviscompany.com

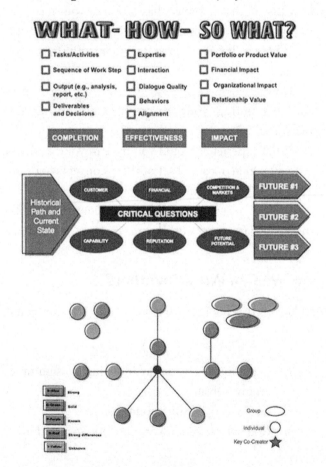

FIVE QUESTIONS TOOL

1. What is **FOUNDATIONAL** in the person's background?	• Early and family life and where • Education and studies • Work—organizations and roles • Life experiences
2. With what does s/he **IDENTIFY**?	• Personal role (e.g., parent, etc.) • Career role (e.g., physician, scientist, expert, leader, etc.) • Impact (e.g., results, relationships, etc.) • Process (e.g. operational, communication, etc.)
3. What **KIND OF PERSON** is s/he?	• When and how s/he works • Patterns of speech • Patterns of action • How s/he thinks
4. What is **IMPORTANT** to him/her?	• In life • For career • As an outcome • In the process
5. What are his/her **INTERESTS**?	• Person hobbies and activities • Areas for learning and exploration

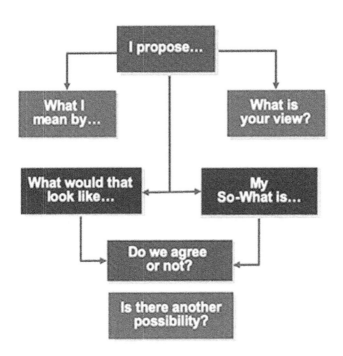

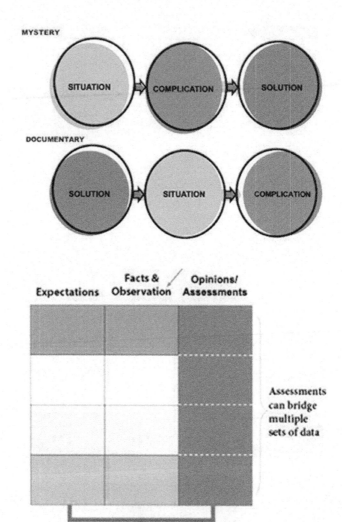

About the Author

Mary Mavis is an executive coach to leaders and teams. She has more than thirty years of experience working inside companies and as an external advisor. She has implemented organizational change and built exceptional talent and team cultures across industries. Mary takes a strong "outcomes" focus to each engagement with a person or team. Her role as a coach, teacher, and consultant is greatly enhanced by a proprietary set of Possibility Thinker Tools™. You can find out more about her work at www.maviscompany.com.

Made in the USA
Coppell, TX
14 January 2022